SECRET WORLD of BUTTERFLIES

COURTNEY SINA MEREDITH • GISELLE CLARKSON

Tāmaki
Paenga Hira
Auckland
War Memorial
Museum

ALLEN&UNWIN
SYDNEY • MELBOURNE • AUCKLAND • LONDON

Butterflies can be big

and butterflies can be teeny.

Fresh out of the chrysalis,

The first poo a butterfly ever does is red and sloppy.

butterflies are wet and wrinkly.

They bask in the sun to dry,
then it's time to feed and fly.

Some soar as high as towers and planes.

Some drink puddles of mud and rain.

Butterflies have special sight.

We see like this.

Flowers look different to their eyes.

We think butterflies
see like this.

At night between rocks and under leaves,
butterflies rest while you're asleep.

Some shine with iridescent wings,

while others are very dark.

Some glide the luscious Amazon,

while others zip around the park.

They're drinking fermented banana juice!

Butterflies love sweet nectar
and they taste with their feet.

If they're drinking crocodile tears,

leave them to their feast!

Some butterflies are see-through,
with wings like panes of glass.

Some butterflies are crafty,

with wings of camouflage.

Try to find them in the mountains,

in the forest and the garden.

Maybe if you're very still,

a butterfly will land on you!

With wings stretched wide, the female Queen Alexandra's birdwing butterfly has a humungous wingspan of up to 32 centimetres – that's as big as a chihuahua! This one is the slightly smaller male. The world's smallest butterfly is the western pygmy blue, which has a teeny-tiny wingspan of 1.5 centimetres – about the size of a peanut.

What is the first thing freshly hatched butterflies do? A sloppy dark-red poo called meconium.

The first poo a butterfly ever does is red and sloppy

When they're too cold to fly butterflies seek a warm place to hang out. This southern blue is sunbathing on a scree pea plant.

Migrating monarchs flit and fly high in the sky, passing glider planes. Pilots have spotted them at heights of more than a kilometre from the ground.

It's mostly male butterflies that gather in groups around smelly mud puddles and pongy pools of pee, searching for salts and minerals to slurp. This is called mud-puddling.

Butterflies have thousands of eyes, and their vision is different from yours and mine. They can see colours and star-like patterns on flowers that we can't. These are called nectar guides and help butterflies to find food.

We see like this.   We think butterflies see like this.

FUN FACTS

The transparent wings of graceful glasswing butterflies help them hide from predators' eyes.

Some butterflies have wings that look like things in their habitat. This clever survival trick is called camouflage.

Butterflies live in all sorts of places, from the alpine meadow home of the Rocky Mountain Apollo (left) to your back garden where the cabbage white thrives (bottom right).

Wouldn't it be fun if a cluster of butterflies clung to you? This is what migrating monarchs do when they make their winter homes in the forests of Mexico. Thousands of butterflies cling to each tree to keep warm.

Thank you to Ray Shannon, whose collection of butterflies inspired the exhibition that inspired this book.

Special thanks also to John Early, Kelly Hall, Ruby Moore and the LA Spedding Bequest.

First published in 2018

Main text copyright © Courtney Sina Meredith, 2018
Fun facts copyright © Auckland Museum, 2018
Illustrations copyright © Giselle Clarkson, 2018

The moral rights of the authors and illustrator have been asserted.

Allen & Unwin
Auckland • Sydney • Melbourne • London
Email: info@allenandunwin.com
Web: www.allenandunwin.co.nz

A catalogue record for this book is available from the National Library of New Zealand

ISBN 978 1 760633 60 8
UK ISBN 978 1 760635 30 5

Design by Kate Barraclough
Set in 19 pt Gotham

Printed and bound in China by Hang Tai Printing Company Limited

10 9 8 7 6 5 4 3 2 1

Published in partnership with Auckland Museum to accompany the exhibition *Secret World of Butterflies* (June 2018 – May 2019), generously supported by the RT Shannon Memorial Trust.

When night falls, butterflies search for a safe roost to rest. They close their wings and go quiet, but no one knows if they 'sleep' in the same way that we do.

The Isabella's longwing butterfly is tiger-striped, as are 200 other species in the Amazon. Some are poisonous and some pretend to be. The copycats use mimicry to fool predators into thinking they're poisonous.

Wondrous butterfly wings are covered in layers of tiny scales. Some scales are coloured with natural pigment. Others reflect light, creating a shimmery shine called iridescence.

Julia butterflies from Brazil are the meanies of the butterfly world, tickling the eyes of the yellow-throated caiman until it cries. They do this so they can slurp up the good stuff in the crocodile's tears.

Some butterflies are super speedy, like this skipper. They zip and skip about at 50 kilometres per hour – that's as fast as a cat can run!

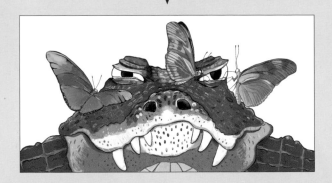

Most butterflies sip sweet nectar from flowers, but these owl butterflies love stinky over-ripe fruit. Drinking fizzy fermented fruit juice is the butterfly version of having a beer!